D0618370

TINY CREEPY CRAWLERS

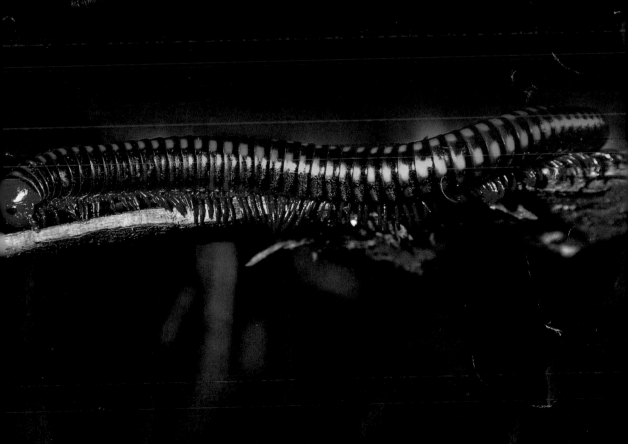

Thanks to the creative team:
Senior Editor: Alice Peebles
Fact checking: Kate Mitchell
Designer: www.collaborate.agency

Hungry Tomato™
A division of Lerner Publishing Group, Inc.
241 First Avenue North
Minneapolis, MN 55401 USA

For reading levels and more information, look up this title at
www.lernerbooks.com.

Main body text set in Calisto MT Regular 12/13.
Typeface provided by Adobe Systems.

Library of Congress Cataloging-in-Publication Data

Names: Turner, Matt, 1964– author. | Calle, Santiago, illustrator. |
Turner, Matt, 1964– Crazy creepy crawlers.
Title: Tiny creepy crawlers / Matt Turner ; Santiago Calle, illustrator.
Description: Minneapolis : Hungry Tomato, [2017] | Series: Crazy
creepy crawlers | Includes index.
Identifiers: LCCN 2016022390 (print) | LCCN 2016024498 (ebook) |
ISBN 9781512415551 (lb : alk. paper) | ISBN 9781512430820 (pb : alk.
paper) | ISBN 9781512427158 (eb pdf)
Subjects: LCSH: Invertebrates—Juvenile literature. | Arthropoda—
Juvenile literature.
Classification: LCC QL362.4 .T87 2017 (print) | LCC QL362.4 (ebook)
| DDC 595—dc23

LC record available at https://lccn.loc.gov/2016022390

Manufactured in the United States of America
1-39915-21385-8/2/2016

CRAZY CREEPY CRAWLERS

TINY CREEPY CRAWLERS

by Matt Turner

Illustrated by Santiago Calle

HUNGRY
TOMATO.

CONTENTS

TINY CREEPY CRAWLERS

Don't be fooled by size. Some of the most powerful creatures are also the smallest! You can find lots of these tiny creatures in your own homes, but others are so small you need a microscope to study them. But despite their small size, all have powers of some sort, including amazing defenses, impressive speed, and the ability to survive in extreme environments.

Tardigrade

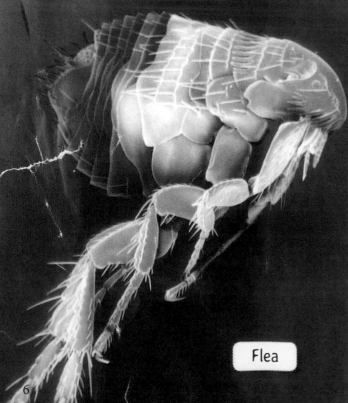

Flea

Unfortunately, when we look on the small scale, we find a lot of unpleasant creatures too. Parasites, such as fleas and worms, live on or in the body of a "host" animal, usually at the host's discomfort. Up to fifty percent of all animal species are parasitic in some way. It's a good life for the parasite, after all, offering easy food and lots of protection.

Tick

Woodlouse

Giant millipede

A few of these parasites, such as the flea and tick, live on our bodies. One or two of them live inside us. And then there are truly troublesome life forms, such as plague bacteria, which are so small they can be passed on in the bodies of tiny parasites—and yet are so deadly that they have changed the course of human history. Mini bugs rule!

TOUGH CRITTERS

Tardigrade means "slow walker." Tardigrades use hydraulics (body fluid pressure) to bend their legs, which are tipped with sharp, curving claws.

When there's no water, tardigrades dry out. In this state they are called tuns, and a sugar called trehalose replaces water in the body to preserve the cells.

Tuns usually survive drying out. They and their eggs may be carried on the wind to new places to start new populations once they're moistened again.

In temperature tests, tardigrades have survived temperatures from −458° to 300° Fahrenheit (−272° to 149° Celsius) . . . way beyond human endurance!

In 2007, the European Space Agency sent tuns and eggs up on a rocket to expose them to the vacuum of space. They were also exposed to levels of solar radiation that would kill humans. After returning to Earth ten days later and being rehydrated, two-thirds of the tuns survived the trip unharmed.

TARDIGRADES

The tiny tardigrade, or water bear, clambers through damp plants, eating tinier animals or algae with its pump-action snout. And it's the toughest animal ever! In tests it has survived being boiled, frozen, pressurized, oxygen-starved, and blitzed with radiation. But its best trick, used when there's no water, is to go into a tun state, where it shrivels like a dry sponge and simply waits—for years, sometimes—to be wet again.

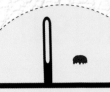

TARDIGRADES
PHYLUM *TARDIGRADA*
Lifespan: ten years or more
Size: 0.004–0.06 inches
(0.1–1.5 millimeters)

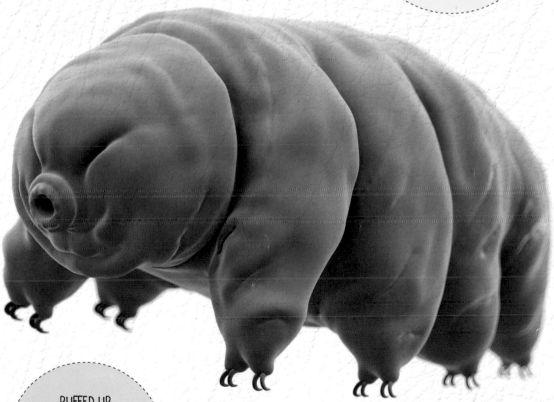

PUFFED UP
When starved of oxygen, tardigrades swell up *(above)* until oxygen levels return to normal. This puffy state is called anoxybiosis.

ALIENS
People have suggested tardigrades might be aliens from another planet. But as they can go without oxygen for only a few days, this isn't likely.

SURVIVORS
Tardigrades can survive pressure almost six times greater than that found in the deepest ocean trenches.

ANCIENT KILLERS

"Yo, bro, from long ago."

"I'm armed and dangerous!"

The velvet worm group—the *Onychophora*—is very, very old. Fossil ancestors have been found that are half a billion years old.

Near a velvet worm's mouth there are two movable turrets known as oral papillae. These face-guns squirt jets of slime up to 12 inches (30 centimeters).

"Gotcha— with both barrels!"

Velvet worms eat woodlice, spiders, crickets, and more. After sneaking up quietly on prey, a velvet worm slimes it to prevent escape. Then it uses the blade-like teeth in its powerful jaws to chomp a hole in the body. Finally, it injects the victim with saliva, which turns the guts into a goo it can suck up.

"Oof! Those old clothes were getting tight."

"Hi Mum!"

Instead of a tough outer skeleton, velvet worms have a soft covering called the cuticula. To grow, they shed the cuticula every couple of weeks.

Some species lay eggs. In others, after a pregnancy of up to fifteen months, a female gives birth to live young that can already look after themselves.

VELVET WORMS

Squashy, leggy, and fuzzy to the touch, the velvet worm is not a worm but a member of an ancient group of deadly predators. Living in damp leaf litter, it stalks a victim in total darkness, tapping it softly with its antennae to see if it's worth attacking. Then—splat!—the velvet worm shoots twin jets of slime from its face-guns, leaving the victim helpless to defend itself.

PERIPATUS
PHYLUM *ONYCHOPHORA*
Lifespan: up to six years
Size: 0.6–6 inches (15–150 mm)

LOTS OF LEGS
Depending on the species (about 180 worldwide), velvet worms have between 13 and 43 leg pairs, with claws that extend for extra grip on rough ground.

DARK DWELLERS
Velvet worms like darkness partly because they need to be damp in order not to dry out. But if they get too wet, they drown.

HIERARCHY
Sometimes several velvet worms gather to feed—but there's a strict pecking order as to who eats first, starting with the bossiest female.

TINY TANKS

Whenever possible, woodlice squeeze their bodies into tight spaces. One desert-dweller stays cool by digging a hole for itself, its partner, and its young.

The sea slater *Ligia oceanica*, a cousin of the woodlouse, lives in the splash zone on the beach. It breathes air, hides in damp cracks, and eats seaweed.

Woodlice of the family *Armadillidae* are known as pillbugs or roly-polies. They can curl their bodies up like a tiny armadillo when threatened. You can find them in the garden. Their body is more rounded than a woodlouse's, but they're easily confused with pill millipedes, which are completely different creatures.

Babies, known as mancas, hatch in a pouch on the mother's underside. A common pillbug (*left*) curls up to release her mancas while a sea slater (*right*) raises her abdomen.

A distant cousin of woodlice is the giant isopod, *Bathynomus giganteus*, which can reach a whopping 14 inches (36 cm)! It is found in cold, deep waters.

WOODLICE

The more than four thousand species of woodlouse and pillbug are crustaceans, cousins of sea creatures like shrimp and crabs. Unlike any other crustacean group, they all live on dry land in all sorts of habitats from deserts to mountains. But there's a chink in their armor: because their exoskeleton isn't waterproof, they can quickly dry out unless they find a dark, damp hiding place—for example, under a plant pot in your backyard.

COMMON WOODLOUSE
ONISCUS ASELLUS
Lifespan: usually two years, but may be up to four
Size: body 0.6 inches (15 mm)

TWO COLORS
Woodlice molt in two stages: first they unshell the back half, then a few days later, the front. That's why you sometimes see two-toned woodlice.

POO!
Woodlice eat their own poop to recycle nutrients. And instead of peeing, they give off ammonia gas. Whew!

STALKING THE SEABED

Attached to the front end of a sea spider are a proboscis (snout), palps, and unusual claw-like organs called chelifores. Not all species have the full kit, though.

The sea spider's abdomen is so thin that it has no room for guts. They're located in the legs! It has no gills either, but takes in oxygen with its exoskeleton.

Long, thin legs are useful for sea spiders that have to wade through seabed muck. Sea spiders in shallower areas tend to have stouter, stronger limbs.

Sea spiders have a pair of ovigers—leg-like limbs that can fold up against the body. Both males and females use these to carry eggs and babies.

Most sea spiders are smaller than a mosquito, but in the waters off Antarctica there are giants measuring up to 24 inches (61 cm) across their legspan, and they rub shoulders with monster worms and crustaceans. It's thought that the high oxygen content of cold water helps support these larger-than-normal life forms.

SEA SPIDERS

With their eight legs, sea spiders may look like land spiders, but they're a completely unrelated group of ancient marine arthropods. They are found worldwide in shallow waters and deep ocean trenches. All sea spiders are scavengers or predators, with a long sharp snout for sucking a snack from the bodies of sea anemones and other seabed life. And, with a few exceptions, they're all unbelievably thin!

SEA SPIDERS
CLASS *PYCOGONIDA*
Lifespan: not known
Size: legspan 0.02–24 inches
(0.5 mm–61 cm)

NO BREATHING
A typical sea spider is so skinny, it has no room for lungs or gills, so it doesn't breathe. Instead, the body absorbs oxygen directly from seawater.

TINY MUSCLES
The leg muscles of some sea spiders are microscopically small: they are formed from a single cell.

Skin Crawlers

There are two main types of louse. Some suck blood and other body fluids, and others nibble on skin, feathers, and dried blood.

One bird, the hooded pitohui of New Guinea, has toxic feathers and skin. Scientists think this may be an adaptation for keeping lice away.

Because nits (eggs) and adults cannot survive more than 24 hours away from a host's warmth, lice use spit to glue their nits to hair or feathers.

There are flies that behave like lice. Louse flies have small (or no) wings but cling tightly to their host—such as a dog or bat—and suck its blood.

During World War I, thousands of soldiers suffered trench fever, a bacterial disease spread by lice that infested their clothing. Symptoms included a fever, headaches, and leg pains. A favorite pastime was squishing the lice in their shirts.

LICE

Almost all mammals have something unpleasant in common: lice! There are around five thousand species of these tiny, wingless insects, and all are ectoparasites. They cling tightly to the skin or hair of a host and feed either by sucking its warm blood or chewing bits of dead skin. Humans are host to three species, which lay their nits (eggs) in our hair and on our clothes. Are you itchy yet?

HUMAN HEAD LOUSE
PEDICULUS HUMANUS CAPITIS
Lifespan: Thirty days from egg to death
Size: 0.09–0.1 inches (2.3–2.5 mm)

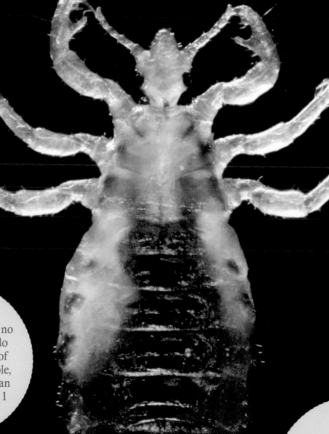

PARASITES
Bats and whales have no insect lice, but they do have other parasites of their own. For example, whales have crustacean lice measuring up to 1 inch (2.5 cm) long.

NITS
Lice have probably always plagued humans. When archaeologists opened 3,000-year-old Egyptian tombs, they found nits on mummies.

CHAMPION JUMPERS

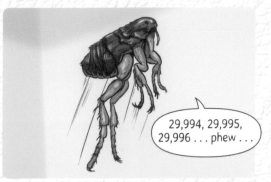

Ever seen a flea going backward? Nope. Backward-pointing bristles on its body help it to push constantly—and rapidly—forward.

A flea can jump 30,000 times nonstop! It jumps by flexing a pad of resilin (a highly elastic protein), then releasing the energy through its legs.

Flea eggs, laid on a host, hatch into legless larvae, which eat the dried blood in the poop of adult fleas. Eggs and larvae may drop off a host at any time. The larva later pupates (develops inside a pupa), often resting in a carpet for months until a host walks near. Then it suddenly springs out to jump onboard.

Fleas breed so fast that, in just three weeks, a single adult pair can populate your pet with a thousand more fleas.

In 1330–1353, a plague known as the Black Death killed more than 75 million people worldwide. The bacterium responsible was carried by fleas on rats.

FLEAS

These little wingless insects, tormentors of your pet cat or dog (or you), are perfectly designed. Powerful hind limbs launch them onto a host, and needle-like mouthparts stab the skin to release blood. Like lice, fleas need their hosts. Hatched adults only live for a few days without feeding, so they snuggle in tight, and their slim, armor-plated bodies are almost impossible to dislodge or crush.

CAT FLEA
CTENOCEPHALIDES FELIS
Lifespan: one month or more, depending on conditions
Size: 0.03–0.07 inches
(0.8–1.8 mm)

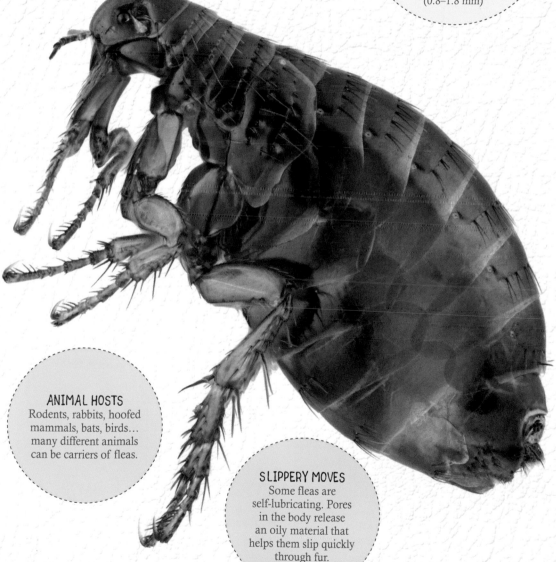

ANIMAL HOSTS
Rodents, rabbits, hoofed mammals, bats, birds… many different animals can be carriers of fleas.

SLIPPERY MOVES
Some fleas are self-lubricating. Pores in the body release an oily material that helps them slip quickly through fur.

Making You Itch

Mites infest animals of all sizes, from elephants to ants. These mites are using their ant host to hitch a ride to somewhere new.

Dust mites love living in our pillows, where they can eat flakes of dead skin. Their poop can cause allergic reactions that make people sneeze and cough.

To get blood from a host, such as a deer, a tick latches onto the body and bites into the skin. As it drinks, its abdomen swells up and darkens. After a female has fed, she drops to the ground and lays her eggs.

A tick can taste with its toes. It does this with an olfactory organ (known as Haller's organ) located in each of its front two feet.

Ticks spread serious diseases. Lyme disease, a bacterial infection that leaves you feeling stiff and tired (sometimes for years), is spread by the deer tick.

MITES AND TICKS

Both these creatures are eight-legged cousins of the spiders. Mites are found all over the world, and even in your bed—though you need a microscope to see them. Some eat organic matter (dead or living plants, dandruff, earwax…). Others are parasites on plants or on all kinds of animals, including humans. They burrow into the skin, feed on tissue and fluids, and cause misery. Ticks are easier to see—they are basically large mites.

MITE
SUBCLASS *ACARI*
Lifespan: usually one month
Size: from microscopic
up to 0.4 inches (10 mm)

SKIN DISEASE
If you see a homeless dog scratching at rough, bare patches of skin, it's probably suffering from mange—an infection caused by mites.

HUMAN CONTACT
You can pick up ticks yourself from a walk in long grass. They must be removed carefully so that the head isn't left buried in the skin.

SURVIVAL TRICKS

In defense, millipedes may coil up into a whorl, protecting the head. The masters at this are the pill millipedes, which look like pillbugs *(page 12)*.

Many millipedes deter predators by oozing bad-tasting chemicals. Motyxia species glow, which is thought to be a warning that they contain cyanide.

Meerkats and coatis are mammals that eat millipedes. They roll them on the ground to "detox" them first. And some monkeys rub the chemicals into their coats as a knockout mosquito repellent!

Some soft-bodied millipedes have tufts of barbed bristles, which they wipe off against enemies, such as ants, to tangle them up.

Millipedes have been known to cause train crashes by swarming over railroad tracks. When the wheels squish the millipedes, the trains slip and derail.

MILLIPEDES

These harmless vegetarians feed on decaying matter on the forest floor, ooching along by means of waves that ripple along their many legs. Harmless? Well, not quite. To fend off predators, they can ooze—or, in some cases, squirt—such nasty toxins as hydrogen cyanide, hydrochloric acid, and benzoquinones, which can burn your skin and dye it brown. Handle with care!

MILLIPEDE
CLASS *DIPLOPODA*
Lifespan: up to ten years or more
Size: 0.03–15 inches
(0.8–381 mm)

LEG COUNT
Millipedes are diplopods, with two pairs of legs per body segment. Depending on the species, they can have from 24 to 750 legs.

FOSSIL PROOF
Fossils with ozopores —the tiny holes from which millipedes leak their toxins—prove these chemical defenses are at least 420 million years old.

Leggy Hunters

Centipedes like to be in tight spaces: they are happiest when both their upper and lower surfaces are touching something firm.

Centipedes don't mind a bit of cannibalism and will gladly eat other centipedes, especially if they find an injured one that cannot escape.

Some centipedes can raise their forequarters into the air and catch bees or wasps in flight! The Peruvian giant centipede is a 12-inch-long (30 cm) monster that has perfected the art of hanging from cave roofs. Despite having poor eyesight, it can catch bats in flight as they leave their roosts in the evening.

Many centipedes are model parents. For example, a mother may lick her eggs to keep them free of fungi or curl her body protectively around hatchlings.

If caught by the legs, a centipede can drop them. While the wriggling legs distract the attacker, the animal escapes. New legs grow after molting.

CENTIPEDES

Running on up to 360 legs, centipedes are superfast, fleeing from view if you uncover them in the yard. Sunlight dries them, so they usually spend the day in a moist hiding place and come out at night to hunt. Armed with venom-packed pincers, centipedes prey on anything they can catch. Small species hunt flies and beetles, and tropical giants may tackle birds, lizards, and mice—and give humans a nasty bite, too.

CENTIPEDE
CLASS *CHILOPODA*
Lifespan: up to ten years
Size: 0.4–12 inches (10–305 mm)

HYGIENE
After feeding, centipedes carefully clean their antennae and legs—all of them!—by running them through their mouthparts.

IN A DASH
The American house centipede can cover 16 inches (40 cm) in a second. That's more than ten body lengths!

An Incredible Journey

The liver fluke's life cycle begins when an adult, living in a mammal's liver, sheds eggs. These come out in the mammal's droppings, such as a cowpat.

A snail eats some cow poop and, with it, some fluke eggs. The eggs then develop into tiny forms called cercariae, which multiply inside the snail.

Irritated by the cercariae, the snail coughs them up in a slime ball, which is later discovered by an ant. The thirsty ant consumes some slime and, with it, some cercariae. These travel into the ant's brain and control its behavior so that it becomes a mindless zombie.

Every evening, the ant climbs a blade of grass and grips the tip with its teeth, then just sits there. Hours later, it returns to its colony but repeats this night after night.

Eventually, a cow chomps the grass stem and swallows the ant with its parasitic cargo. The adult flukes develop and burrow into the cow's liver to lay eggs of their own.

LIVER FLUKE

Flukes are also known as flatworms and belong to a group called the trematodes. They are parasites that enter the guts of snails, fish, and birds as well as sheep or cattle, where they feast on the host's body fluids. Flukes can make livestock so sickly that farmers sometimes lose entire herds. How the flatworms enter those bodies is truly astonishing as it involves not one, but several hosts.

LANCET LIVER FLUKE
DICROCOELIUM DENDRITICUM
Lifespan: dependent on host
Size: adult up to
0.6 inches (15 mm)

INFESTATIONS
Humans can suffer from fluke infestations too. One way to get them is by eating unwashed watercress or undercooked meat.

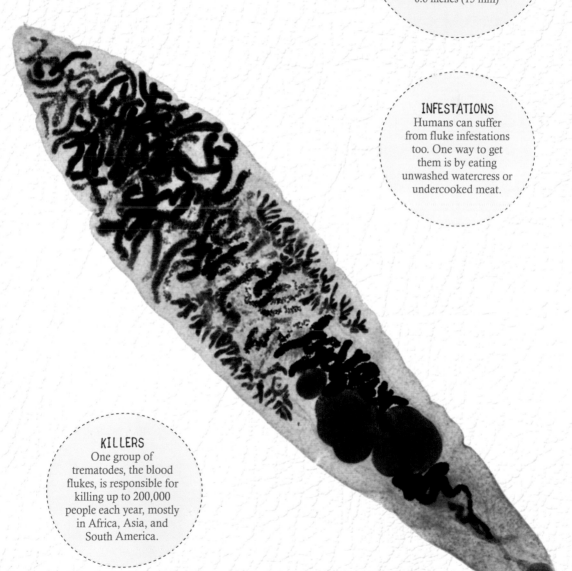

KILLERS
One group of trematodes, the blood flukes, is responsible for killing up to 200,000 people each year, mostly in Africa, Asia, and South America.

MINI CREATURES

Mini bugs, though small, have some standout qualities—whether it's their size, their lifestyle, or simply how long they've been around on Earth.

Mini-pede:
The smallest millipede is probably the bristly millipede *Polyxenus lagurus*, found in North America and Europe. Measuring just 0.1 inches (2.5 mm) long, it can shed hairs in self-defense. The longest is probably *Archispirostreptus gigas* of East Africa *(left)*, which can reach 15 inches (381 mm). The record for most legs—of any animal—goes to the tiny *Illacme plenipes* of California, which has up to 750 legs but measures barely 1 inch (25 mm) long.

Mite be useful: The mites on this sexton beetle are hitching a ride—and the host puts up with them because they're useful. The beetle lays its eggs in animal carcasses, such as dead mice, for its babies to feed on. The mites can usually be relied on to eat the eggs and larvae of any other species (such as a fly) that has reached the carcass first.

BOING!

Super slimy:

Planarians are a group of predatory flatworms. Some species live in water while others live on land, where they move like slugs on a layer of slime. If a planarian is cut into pieces, each piece grows back all of its missing parts to become a complete individual. Even if you chop the head off, it'll grow a whole new body. How's that for a super power!

Micro-shrimp:

These fingernail-sized crustaceans are brine shrimps. Their cysts (eggs), which can wait for up to twenty-five years before hatching into healthy larvae, are cultivated widely for use as farmed fish food. Like water bears, brine shrimps have been sent into space, but with a much lower survival rate.

Earliest insects:

This ancient dragonfly is trapped in amber. Its ancestors first appeared around 300 million years ago. They first evolved winged flight about 400 million years ago, which is when land plants began to grow much taller. Scientists think insects and plants evolved together. Today, around sixty-five percent of plants are insect-pollinated.

PARASITES ON PARADE

Many tiny creepy crawlers are parasites: creatures that depend on other creatures for their survival—perhaps to gain free food or shelter. Below are a couple more parasites you may find interesting . . .

Leeches

Leeches are segmented worms with a sucker at each end of a muscular, stretchy body. With around 680 species known worldwide, they range from 0.3 to 12 inches (8 to 305 mm). Most live in freshwater, where they latch onto almost any creature—living or dead—to suck its fluids. They often go for snails, but if you're unlucky, a leech may find you. If you don't remove it first, it'll drop off after drinking its fill of blood.

When biting, leeches inject a chemical called hirudin that prevents blood from clotting, so wounds can leak for hours after the leech has been removed. For more than 2,000 years, drawing blood was a common cure for a wide range of ailments, and doctors put leeches on their patients to do the bloodletting. Some still do!

Tapeworms

Tapeworms belong to a group called the *platyhelminthes* (meaning *flatworms*). One type commonly found in humans is *Diphyllobothrium*, which you can pick up by eating raw or undercooked fish infested with the tapeworm larvae. The tapeworm then grows in your gut, where it feeds by absorbing nutrients. In other words, it eats your food. Tapeworms don't really qualify as *tiny*, given that they can rapidly grow to terrifying lengths. One of the longest ever found in a human gut was 82 feet (25 meters) long! But don't worry: you can usually get rid of them with pills.

GLOSSARY

abdomen
the hind part of an insect's three-part body

arthropod
member of the group that includes crustaceans, insects, myriapods (centipedes, millipedes, and so on), and spiders. The word means *jointed leg*.

bacterium
a microscopically small life form, often occurring in soil or water in large numbers, and often capable of causing sickness or disease. The plural of bacterium is *bacteria*.

class
a large group of animals of a similar type, such as *Mammalia* (mammals)

crustacean
a member of a group of animals including barnacles, crabs, lobsters, and shrimp. Most are marine animals, but some, such as woodlice, live on land.

exoskeleton
the shell or outer casing that provides structural strength and protection for an arthropod, in place of an internal skeleton. The exoskeleton must be molted regularly for an animal to grow.

larva
a juvenile that hatches from the egg and later transforms into a pupa, or directly into an adult. The plural of larva is *larvae*.

molt
in insects, to shed the hard exoskeleton (outer part) in order to grow

olfactory
the sensory system used for the sense of smell

papilla
a tiny, rounded bump on a surface, often having a sensory function. Your tongue, for example, is covered with papillae—these are the taste buds. The plural of papilla is *papillae*.

parasite
a life form that spends all or part of its life cycle on or inside another life form, known as the host. An obligate parasite cannot survive away from its host. An ectoparasite lives on the outside (skin, fur, and so on) while an endoparasite lives on the inside, often in the digestive system.

phylum
a very large group of animals, each containing different classes. Mammals belong to a phylum called *chordates*.

predator
an animal that kills and eats other animals. Roughly one-third of all insect species are predators.

pupate
to transform into a pupa, a stage of development in which the insect larva rests inside a case and gradually transforms into an adult

species
a type of animal or plant (or other life form). Members of a species are defined as a group of individuals that are similar enough to be able to breed and produce fertile offspring.

vacuum
a space that contains no air and therefore no air pressure

INDEX

The Author

British-born Matt Turner graduated from Loughborough College of Art in the 1980s. Since then he has worked as a photo researcher, editor, and writer. He has written books on diverse topics including natural history, earth sciences, and railways as well as hundreds of articles for encyclopedias and partworks, covering everything from elephants to abstract art. He and his family currently live in Auckland, Aotearoa/New Zealand, where he volunteers for the local coast guard unit and dabbles in painting.

The Artist

Born in Medellín, Colombia, Santiago Calle is an illustrator and animator trained at Edinburgh College of Art in the UK. He began his career as a teacher, which led him to deepen his studies in sequential art. Santiago partnered with his brother Juan to found his art studio, Liberum Donum, in Bogotá in 2006. Since then, they have dedicated themselves to producing concept art, illustration, comic strip art, and animation.

Picture Credits (abbreviations: t = top; b = bottom; c = center; l = left; r = right)
© www.shutterstock.com:
1 c, 2 cl, 4 c, 6 tr, 6 bl, 7 tl, 7 tr, 7 b, 9 c, 11 c, 13 c, 15 c, 19 c, 21 c, 23 c, 25 c, 27 c, 28 tl, 28 br, 29 tl, 29 cr, 29 bl, 32 cr.

17 c © CDC/ Frank Collins, Ph.D / James Gathany